Plant Growth and Reproduction

Lesson 1

How Do Plants Grow?............................ 2

Lesson 2

How Do Plants Reproduce? 10

Harcourt
SCHOOL PUBLISHERS

Orlando   Austin   New York   San Diego   Toronto   London

Visit *The Learning Site!*
www.harcourtschool.com

Lesson 1

How Do Plants Grow?

VOCABULARY
vascular tissue
xylem
phloem
photosynthesis

Vascular plants, like trees, have vascular tissue. **Vascular tissue** carries water and food. Roots, stems, and leaves have vascular tissue.

xylem

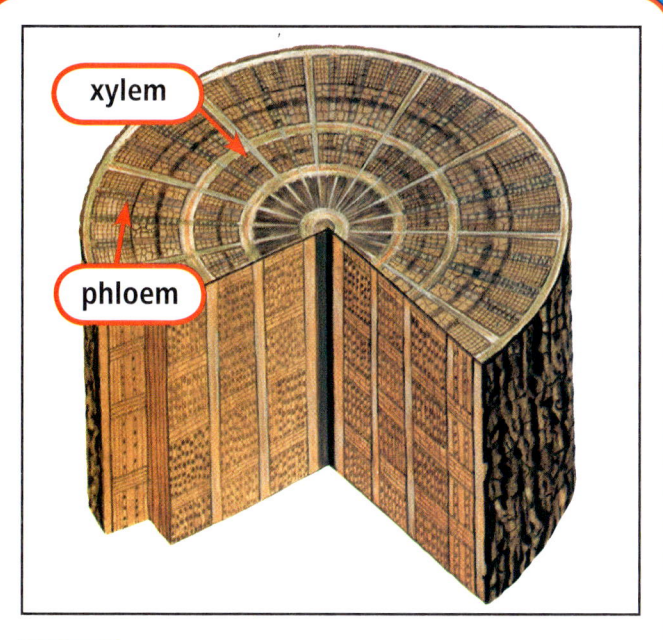

phloem

Xylem is vascular tissue. It carries water and nutrients from the roots to other parts of the plant. **Phloem** is also vascular tissue. It carries food from leaves to the rest of the plant.

Photosynthesis is the process by which plants make food. Photosynthesis takes places inside leaves.

> **READING FOCUS SKILL**
> **MAIN IDEA AND DETAILS**
> The main idea is the most important idea in what you read. Details are smaller pieces of information about the main idea.
>
> As you read, look for details about plant structure and function.

Nonvascular Plants

Some plants do not have tubes to carry food and water. Instead, they absorb water and nutrients from their surroundings. These plants are called nonvascular plants.

Nonvascular plants do not have true roots. Instead, they have small rootlike structures. The structures help to keep the plants in place.

Nonvascular plants do not have true stems or leaves. However, they have small leaflike structures that make food. These aren't true leaves because they don't have tubes to carry materials.

Instead, water and nutrients move from cell to cell. Nonvascular plants do not grow very tall. Their small size allows them to absorb all the water they need.

Focus Skill: Tell why the leaflike structures of nonvascular plants are not true leaves.

Moss is a nonvascular plant that often grows on rocks and trees.

Vascular Plants

Trees belong to a group of plants called vascular plants. Vascular plants contain vascular tissue. **Vascular tissue** helps support plants as they grow upright. It also carries water and food to all parts of the plant.

Vascular plants vary more than nonvascular plants. They include tiny duckweed and giant redwood trees. They also include cacti that grow in dry deserts, and orchids that grow in damp rain forests.

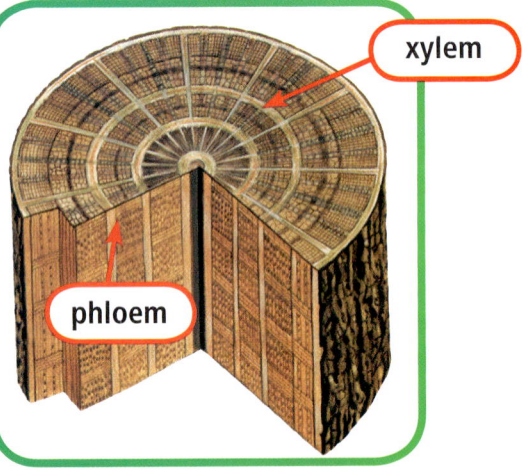

xylem

phloem

There are two types of vascular tissue. **Xylem** carries water and nutrients from the roots. **Phloem** carries food from leaves to all other plant cells.

Vascular plants don't depend on water moving from cell to cell. As a result, they can grow larger.

Tell the difference between xylem and phloem.

Roots

Roots absorb water and nutrients from the soil. Xylem moves water and nutrients from a plant's roots to its stems and leaves.

Roots also help hold the plant in place. Some roots are fibrous. They are thin and branching. Fibrous roots form a mat below the ground. This mat of roots can absorb water from a large area. It also holds the soil in place. Grasses have lots of fibrous roots. They are often used to hold the soil.

Fibrous roots ▲

A taproot is one large root that pushes deep into the ground. Some taproots store food for the plant. The plant uses the stored food when it makes flowers and fruit.

People use some taproots for food. Carrots and beets are examples.

Some roots grow above ground. They are called prop roots. They help hold the plant upright. Corn has prop roots.

Taproot ▲

Name some different kinds of roots and tell what they do.

Stems

Stems usually grow up from the ground. They hold the plant's leaves up in the sunlight.

Stems also carry water and nutrients from roots to leaves. The vascular tissue in stems forms bundles. In some plants, the bundles are scattered throughout the stem. In trees and many woody plants, the bundles form rings.

Stems provide support for plants. Trees and other tall plants have woody cells in their stems. These woody cells make the stems strong.

Tall trees have strong trunks and branches. Trunks and branches are stems.

Focus Skill Tell what stems do for plants.

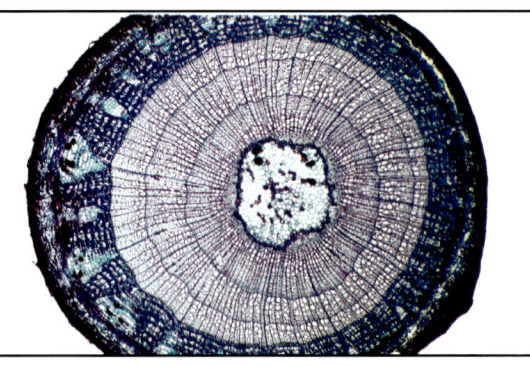

The center of a tree trunk is filled with woody cells. The cells provide support for the tree. The rings are bundles of vascular tissue.

Leaves

Leaves make food by a process called **photosynthesis**. The process uses light energy, carbon dioxide, and water to make sugar.

Photosynthesis takes place inside chloroplasts in leaf cells. A green material called chlorophyll absorbs sunlight. Leaves get carbon dioxide from the air. Xylem in leaf veins moves water from the soil.

Phloem cells carry the sugar from photosynthesis throughout the plant. Oxygen, a waste product, goes into the air.

Leaves need sunlight to make food.

Tell where plants get the things they need to carry out photosynthesis.

Review

Complete this main idea sentence.

1. Nonvascular plants do not contain _____ tissue.

Complete these detail statements.

2. Water in nonvascular plants carries nutrients from _____ to _____.

3. A mat of fibrous roots can absorb _____ from a large area.

4. Photosynthesis takes place inside _____ in leaf cells.

Lesson 2

VOCABULARY
spore
gymnosperm
angiosperm
germinate

How Do Plants Reproduce?

A **spore** is a cell that can grow into a new plant. This close-up of a moss shows spore stalks. Each one is filled with hundreds of spores.

A **gymnosperm** is a plant that produces "naked" seeds. Pine trees are gymnosperms.

A seed **germinates**, or sprouts, when everything is just right for growth. This germinating seed has put out a tiny root.

An **angiosperm** is a plant that produces seeds protected by a fruit. Apple trees are angiosperms.

11

> **READING FOCUS SKILL**
> **COMPARE AND CONTRAST**
> To **compare and contrast** is to show how things are alike and different.
> **Compare and contrast** the ways plants reproduce.

Simple Plants Reproduce

Mosses and ferns reproduce by spores. A **spore** is a single cell. A spore can grow into a new plant.

Both mosses and ferns produce spores. The spores grow into tiny plants called *gametophytes* (guh•MEET•uh•fyts).

The moss plants you see growing on rocks or logs are gametophytes. The gametophytes of ferns are tiny and grow flat on the ground.

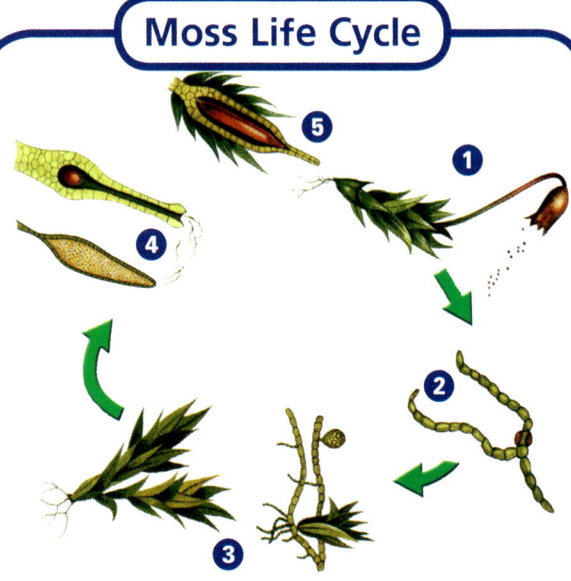

Moss Life Cycle

These spore stalks are growing from moss plants. The stalks are called sporophytes. The plants are called gametophytes.

(1) Spores are released. (2) Gametophytes grow from spores. (3) Structures on female gametophytes produce eggs. Structures on male gametophytes produce sperm. (4) Egg and sperm join. (5) New sporophyte grows.

Gametophytes have both male and female parts. The male cells are called sperm. The female cells are called eggs.

Mosses and ferns need water to reproduce. This allows the sperm to swim to the eggs.

The male and female cells join to become one cell. This process is called fertilization. A fertilized egg grows into a sporophyte, which makes spores. The spores grow into new gametophytes.

Focus Skill **How are mosses and ferns alike? How are they different?**

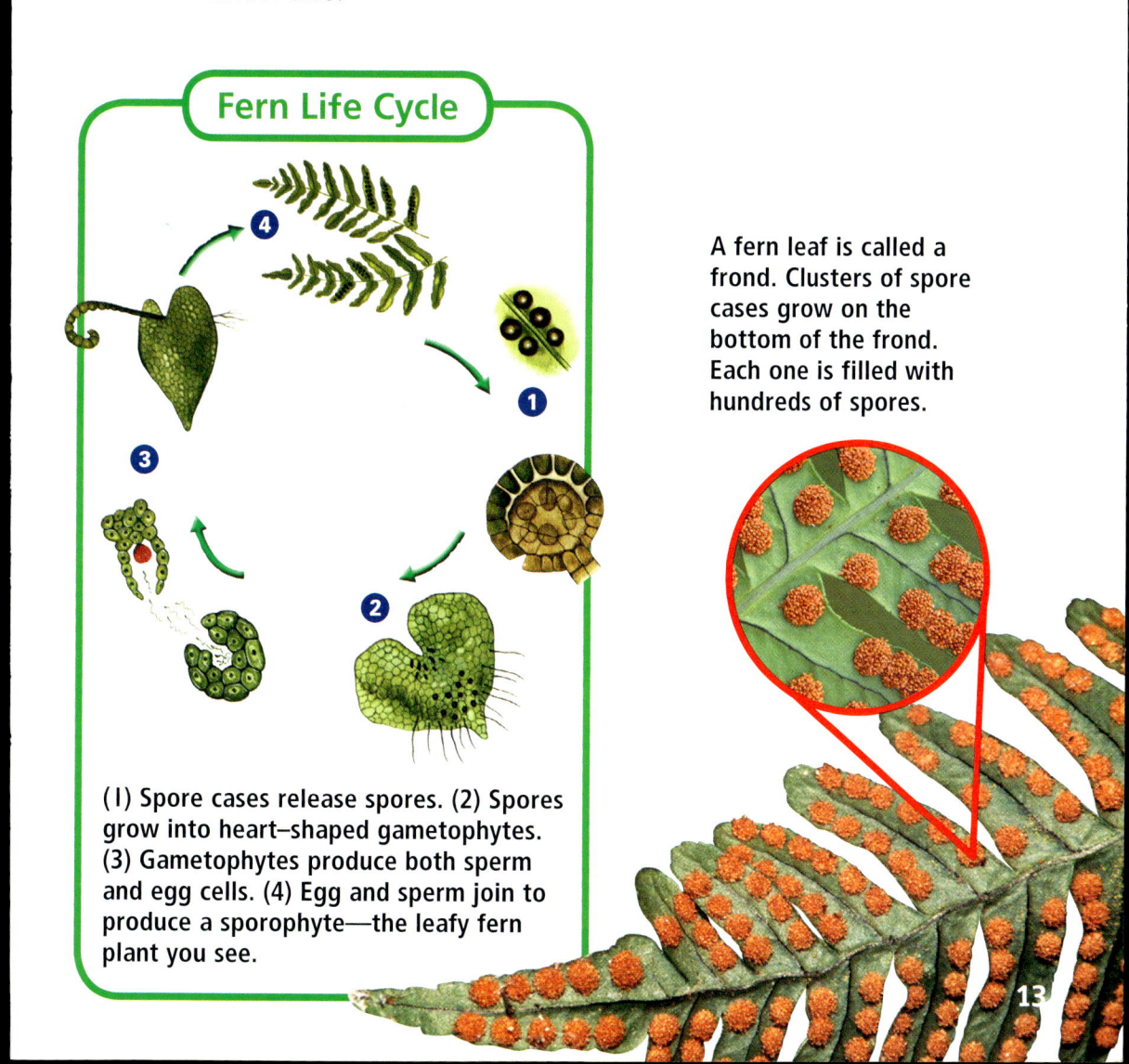

Fern Life Cycle

A fern leaf is called a frond. Clusters of spore cases grow on the bottom of the frond. Each one is filled with hundreds of spores.

(1) Spore cases release spores. (2) Spores grow into heart-shaped gametophytes. (3) Gametophytes produce both sperm and egg cells. (4) Egg and sperm join to produce a sporophyte—the leafy fern plant you see.

Seed–Bearing Plants

Most plants produce seeds. Seed plants don't need water for fertilization. This helps seed plants to grow in many environments.

The seeds of pine trees are called "naked" seeds. They are protected by only a thin seed coat. A plant that produces "naked" seeds is called a **gymnosperm**.

Small, male pine cones produce pollen. Pollen contains sperm cells. Female pine cones are larger than male cones. They grow high in trees above the male cones. Eggs develop on the scales of female cones.

Pine trees produce naked seeds in cones.

Apple seeds grow inside the fruit of the apple, where they are protected.

Male cones release millions of pollen grains. Some of the pollen settles on the scales of female cones. Sperm in the pollen fertilize the eggs. Then seeds begin to grow.

When the seeds are mature, they are released from the cones. The seeds are carried by the wind until they land on the ground. If the conditions are right, the seeds grow into new plants.

Plants that grow flowers are called **angiosperms**. They don't have cones. Instead, they grow seeds inside fruit. The fruit protects the seeds.

Because angiosperms have protected seeds, they live in most parts of the world.

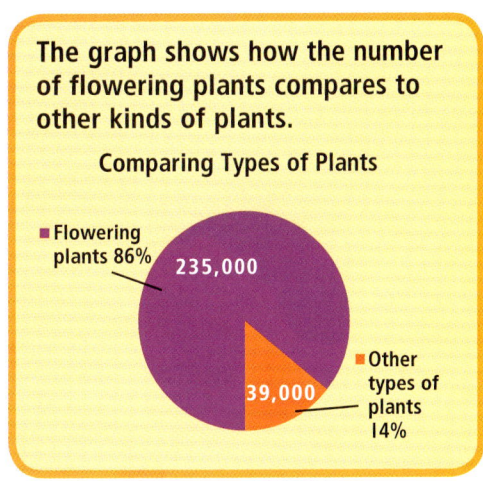

The graph shows how the number of flowering plants compares to other kinds of plants.

Comparing Types of Plants

- Flowering plants 86% — 235,000
- Other types of plants 14% — 39,000

Tell how male and female pine cones are alike and different.

15

Flowers to Seeds

The flower is where fertilization takes place in flowering plants. Male and female parts are often together in the same flower. Pollen comes from the male parts called *anthers*. The female part is called a *stigma*. It is in the center of the flower.

Flowers start as buds. As the buds unfold, they reveal the petals of the flowers. The colors or shape of the petals may attract animals. Some flowers have a scent that attracts animals. Some kinds of flowers attract insects and birds with a sugary nectar.

When a fruit tree is in bloom, insects pollinate the flowers. Sperm in pollen from one flower can fertilize the eggs in other flowers. The eggs become seeds inside the fruit.

Inside a Flower

Look inside a flower to see the parts that work together to make seeds.

Stigma—collects pollen

Anther—makes pollen

Ovary—contains ovules. After fertilization, the ovary develops into a fruit.

Ovules—produce eggs. Eggs are fertilized by sperm from pollen and develop into seeds.

Pollen tube—grows from pollen grain. The tube enables sperm to travel into ovules to fertilize eggs.

Petals—attract insects for pollination

Bees help fertililze many kinds of flowers. Bees climb into flowers to get at the nectar. Pollen from the anthers sticks to the bees' legs. When the bees go to other flowers, some of the pollen on their legs clings to the sticky stigma.

After fertilization, the egg develops into a seed. The seed contains a tiny plant called an *embryo*. The ovary becomes the fruit.

Focus Skill Tell the difference between the stigma of a flower and the anthers of a flower.

Seed Germination

Seeds **germinate**, or sprout, when conditions are right for the embryo to grow. A thick, waxy seed coat protects the embryo until the seed germinates.

Some seeds germinate when there are enough hours of light. Most need to have warm soil in the spring. Seeds also need water.

When the time is right, a seed soaks up water and expands. This breaks the seed coat. The embryo begins to grow. First, the embryo's root grows into the soil. The root takes up water. Next, a shoot pushes up.

A seed contains a tiny embryo. It stays in the ground until conditions are right for the seed to germinate.

After the seed coat splits, the embryo's root begins to grow into the soil. Now the embryo can get water.

Food in the seed feeds the embryo as the shoot grows up toward the light.

The leaves of the embryo can't yet make food. But the embryo needs energy to grow. Tiny structures in the seed called *cotyledons* contain food. This food provides energy until the new plant can make its own food.

The first leaves come up from the ground. Photosynthesis can now take place. The leaves turn green with sunlight. Rapid growth begins. The embryo becomes a seedling.

The stem grows, leaves develop, and roots spread in the soil. Now the seedling can make its own food.

Describe the steps from seed to seedling.

Review

Complete these compare and contrast statements.

1. Mosses grow from _____. Apple trees grow from _____.

2. Plants with naked seeds are called _____. Plants with seeds protected by fruit are called _____.

3. Male cones contain _____. Female cones contain _____.

4. In gymnosperms, seeds develop in _____. In angiosperms, seeds develop in _____.

GLOSSARY

angiosperm (AN•jee•oh•sperm) A flowering plant that has seeds protected by fruit.

germinate (JER•muh•nayt) To sprout.

gymnosperm (JIM•noh•sperm) A plant that produces naked seeds.

phloem (FLOH•em) Vascular tissue that carries food from leaves to all plant cells.

photosynthesis (foht•oh•SIHN•thuh•sis) The process in which plants make food. They use water from the soil, carbon dioxide from the air, and energy from sunlight.

spore (SPAWR) A single cell that can grow into a new plant.

vascular tissue (VAS•kyuh•ler TISH•oo) Tissue that supports plants and carries water and food.

xylem (ZY•luhm) Vascular tissue that carries water and nutrients from roots to other parts of a plant.